M000046503

To: _Debi_

From: _Bev_

A Little Book of

Lve

©2010 Freeman-Smith, LLC.
All rights reserved. Except for brief quotations used in reviews, articles, or other media, no part of this book may be reproduced or transmitted in any form or by any means, electronic or mechanical, including photocopying, recording, or by information storage or retrieval system, without permission by the publisher.

Freeman-Smith, LLC.
Nashville, TN 37202

The quoted ideas expressed in this book (but not Scripture verses) are not, in all cases, exact quotations, as some have been edited for clarity and brevity. In all cases, the author has attempted to maintain the speaker's original intent. In some cases, quoted material for this book was obtained from secondary sources, primarily print media. While every effort was made to ensure the accuracy of these sources, the accuracy cannot be guaranteed. For additions, deletions, corrections, or clarifications in future editions of this text, please write Freeman-Smith, LLC.

The Holy Bible, King James Version

The Holy Bible, New King James Version (NKJV) Copyright © 1982 by Thomas Nelson, Inc. Used by permission.

The Holman Christian Standard Bible™ (HCSB) Copyright © 1999, 2000, 2001 by Holman Bible Publishers. Used by permission.

Cover Design by Kim Russell / Wahoo Designs
Page Layout by Bart Dawson

ISBN 978-1-60587-232-2

Printed in the United States of America

A Little Book of

L●ve

Table of Contents

*Now these three remain: faith, hope, and love.
But the greatest of these is love.*

—

1 Corinthians 13:13 HCSB

Introduction

"**B**ut the greatest of these is love"—seven familiar words that remind us of a simple truth: God places a high priority on love . . . and so should we. Faith is important, of course. So too is hope. But love is more important still.

Christ demonstrated His love for us on the cross, and, as Christians, we are called upon to return Christ's love by sharing it. We are commanded to love one another just as Christ loved us (John 13:34). That's a simple commandment to understand, but a difficult commandment to put into practice, especially when we're tired, frustrated, confused, or worried. But with Christ as our guide, we can demonstrate our love for others, even on those difficult days when we might prefer to do otherwise.

So do yourself (and your loved ones) a favor: take these ideas to heart and weave them into the fabric of your relationships. When you do, you'll learn firsthand the truth of God's Word: "the greatest of these" is now—and will forever be—love.

Chapter 1

Love Is . . .

*Dear friends, if God loved us in this way,
we also must love one another.*

—

1 John 4:11 HCSB

How do you define love? Is it simply a warm feeling that you feel in the pit of your stomach, or is it something more? Is it a fleeting burst of emotions that may be here today and gone tomorrow, or is it something more? Is love merely a strong physical attraction that you feel towards a person whose appearance you admire, or is it something more? If you answered "something more," you're right. Feelings of infatuation come and go, but genuine love isn't like that—real love lasts.

Genuine love is patient, understanding, consistent, and considerate. Genuine love doesn't just sit around and do nothing; it is translated into acts of kindness. Genuine love doesn't always spring up overnight, but it doesn't vanish overnight, either. And, genuine love requires effort. Simply put, if you wish to build lasting relationships, you must be willing to do your part.

God does not intend for you to experience mediocre relationships; He created you for far greater things. Building lasting relationships requires compassion, wisdom, empathy, kindness, courtesy, and forgiveness (lots of forgiveness). If that sounds a lot like work, it is—which is perfectly fine with God. Why? Because He knows that you are capable of doing that work, and because He knows that the fruits of your labors will enrich the lives of your loved ones and the lives of generations yet unborn.

15

Only joyous love redeems.

—

Catherine Marshall

If Jesus is the preeminent One in our lives, then we will love each other, submit to each other, and treat one another fairly in the Lord.

Warren Wiersbe

16

Those who abandon ship the first time it enters a storm miss the calm beyond. And the rougher the storms weathered together, the deeper and stronger real love grows.

Ruth Bell Graham

Love is an attribute of God. To love others is evidence of a genuine faith.

Kay Arthur

Love Is . . .

How do you spell love? When you reach the point where the happiness, security, and development of another person is as much of a driving force to you as your own happiness, security, and development, then you have a mature love. True love is spelled G-I-V-E. It is not based on what you can get, but rooted in what you can give to the other person.

Josh McDowell

17

Love must be supported and fed and protected, just like a little infant who is growing up at home.

James Dobson

Love is the seed of all hope. It is the enticement to trust, to risk, to try, and to go on.

Gloria Gaither

love

It is when we come to the Lord in our nothingness, our power-lessness and our helplessness that He then enables us to love in a way which, without Him, would be absolutely impossible.

Elisabeth Elliot

18

Love simply cannot spring up without that self-surrender to each other. If either withholds the self, love cannot exist.

E. Stanley Jones

Live your lives in love, the same sort of love which Christ gives us, and which He perfectly expressed when He gave Himself as a sacrifice to God.

Corrie ten Boom

To have fallen in love hints to our hearts
that all of earthly life is not hopelessly fallen.
Love is the laughter of God.

—

Beth Moore

19

I pray that you, being rooted and firmly established in love, may be able to comprehend with all the saints what is the breadth and width, height and depth, and to know the Messiah's love that surpasses knowledge, so you may be filled with all the fullness of God.

Ephesians 3:17-19 HCSB

20

If I speak the languages of men and of angels, but do not have love, I am a sounding gong or a clanging cymbal.

1 Corinthians 13:1 HCSB

Dear friends, if God loved us in this way, we also must love one another.

1 John 4:11 HCSB

Love Is . . .

Now the goal of our instruction is love from a pure heart, a good conscience, and a sincere faith.

1 Timothy 1:5 HCSB

Love one another fervently with a pure heart.

1 Peter 1:22 NKJV

Above all, put on love—the perfect bond of unity.

Colossians 3:14 HCSB

And may the Lord cause you to increase and overflow with love for one another and for everyone, just as we also do for you.

1 Thessalonians 3:12 HCSB

We love because He first loved us.

1 John 4:19 HCSB

22

Love is not measured by what it gets,
but by what it costs.

—

Oswald Chambers

Chapter 2

Sharing God's Love

For the Lord is good, and His love is eternal;
His faithfulness endures through all generations.

—

Psalm 100:5 HCSB

Have you built your relationships on the solid foundation of God's love? Is God the foundation upon which you've built your marriage, your family, and your friendships? If so, you are wise, and you are blessed. If not, it's time to reconsider your priorities for life and for love.

God's love for you is deeper and more profound than you can fathom. And now, precisely because you are a wondrous creation treasured by God, a question presents itself: What will you do in response to God's love? Will you ignore it or embrace it? Will you return it or neglect it? The decision, of course, is yours and yours alone.

When you and your loved ones embrace God together, you are forever changed. When you embrace God's love, you feel differently about yourself, your relationships, your family, and your world. When you embrace God's love together, you will share His message, and you will obey His commandments. When you do these things, your love will endure forever.

Sharing God's Love

God is a God of unconditional, unremitting love, a love that corrects and chastens but never ceases.

Kay Arthur

God loves us the way we are, but He loves us too much to leave us that way.

Leighton Ford

Accepting God's love as a gift instead of trying to earn it had somehow seemed presumptuous and arrogant to me, when, in fact, my pride was tricking me into thinking that I could merit His love and forgiveness with my own strength.

Lisa Whelchel

The love of God is revealed in that He laid down His life for His enemies.

Oswald Chambers

It is God to whom and with whom we travel, and while He is the End of our journey, He is also at every stopping place.

Elisabeth Elliot

26

The great love of God is an ocean without a bottom or a shore.

C. H. Spurgeon

God loves each of us as if there were only one of us.

St. Augustine

Jesus loves us with fidelity, purity, constancy, and passion, no matter how imperfect we are.

Stormie Omartian

God's love is measureless. It is more: it is boundless. It has no bounds because it is not a thing but a facet of the essential nature of God. His love is something he is, and because he is infinite, that love can enfold the whole created world in itself and have room for ten thousand times ten thousand worlds beside.

27

A. W. Tozer

As God's children, we are the recipients of lavish love—a love that motivates us to keep trusting even when we have no idea what God is doing.

Beth Moore

For God loved the world in this way: He gave His only Son, so that everyone who believes in Him will not perish but have eternal life.

John 3:16 HCSB

28

[Because of] the Lord's faithful love we do not perish, for His mercies never end. They are new every morning; great is Your faithfulness!

Lamentations 3:22-23 HCSB

Help me, Lord my God; save me according to Your faithful love.

Psalm 109:26 HCSB

Sharing God's Love

Whoever is wise will observe these things, and they will understand the lovingkindness of the Lord.

Psalm 107:43 NKJV

The Lord is gracious and compassionate, slow to anger and great in faithful love. The Lord is good to everyone; His compassion [rests] on all He has made.

Psalm 145:8-9 HCSB

For He is gracious and compassionate, slow to anger, rich in faithful love.

Joel 2:13 HCSB

Though we may not act like our Father,
there is no greater truth than this:
We are his. Unalterably.
He loves us. Undyingly.
Nothing can separate us
from the love of Christ.

—

Max Lucado

30

Chapter 3

Love Is Kind

Just as you want others to do for you, do the same for them.

—

Luke 6:31 HCSB

Never underestimate the power of kindness. You never know what kind word or gesture will significantly change someone's day, or week, or life.

Is your home like the Old West, a place "where never is heard a discouraging word and the skies are not cloudy all day" . . . or is the forecast at your house slightly cloudier than that? If your house is a place where the rule of the day is the Golden Rule, don't change a thing. Kindness starts at home, but it should never end there.

So today, slow yourself down and be alert for those who need your smile, your kind words, or your helping hand. Make kindness a centerpiece of your dealings with others. They will be blessed, and so will you.

If we have the true love of God in our hearts, we will show it in our lives. We will not have to go up and down the earth proclaiming it. We will show it in everything we say or do.

D. L. Moody

When we do little acts of kindness that make life more bearable for someone else, we are walking in love as the Bible commands us.

Barbara Johnson

A little kindly advice is better than a great deal of scolding.

Fanny Crosby

When you extend hospitality to others, you're not trying to impress people, you're trying to reflect God to them.

Max Lucado

Do all the good you can. By all the means you can. In all the ways you can. In all the places you can. At all the times you can. To all the people you can. As long as ever you can.

John Wesley

There are many timid souls whom we jostle morning and evening as we pass them by; but if only the kind word were spoken they might become fully persuaded.

Fanny Crosby

Kindness in this world will do much to help others, not only to come into the light, but also to grow in grace day by day.

Fanny Crosby

Be so preoccupied with good will
that you haven't room for ill will.

—

E. Stanley Jones

35

Finally, all of you be of one mind, having compassion for one another; love as brothers, be tenderhearted, be courteous.

1 Peter 3:8 NKJV

36

Love is patient; love is kind.

1 Corinthians 13:4 HCSB

And may the Lord make you increase and abound in love to one another and to all.

1 Thessalonians 3:12 NKJV

Love Is Kind

And be kind and compassionate to one another, forgiving one another, just as God also forgave you in Christ.

Ephesians 4:32 HCSB

Pure and undefiled religion before our God and Father is this: to look after orphans and widows in their distress and to keep oneself unstained by the world.

James 1:27 HCSB

Carry one another's burdens; in this way you will fulfill the law of Christ.

Galatians 6:2 HCSB

38

When you launch an act of kindness
out into the crosswinds of life,
it will blow kindness back to you.

—

Dennis Swanberg

Chapter 4

Love Is Generous

He has dispersed abroad, He has given to the poor;
His righteousness endures forever;
His horn will be exalted with honor.

—

Psalm 112:9 NKJV

God's Word promises that He rewards generosity. So if we sincerely desire to experience His greatest blessings, we must be generous with our time, our talents, our encouragement, and our possessions. When we become generous ambassadors for God, He blesses us in ways that we cannot fully understand. But if we allow ourselves to become closefisted and miserly, either with our possessions or with our love, we deprive ourselves of the spiritual abundance that would otherwise be ours.

Do you seek God's abundance and His peace? Then share the blessings that God has given you—and teach your family members to do likewise. God expects no less, and He deserves no less. And neither, come to think of it, do your neighbors.

Love Is Generous

We are never more like God than when we give.

Charles Swindoll

The measure of a life, after all, is not its duration but its donation.

Corrie ten Boom

The happiest and most joyful people are those who give money and serve.

Dave Ramsey

Abundant living means abundant giving.

E. Stanley Jones

Here lies the tremendous mystery—that God should be all-powerful, yet refuse to coerce. He summons us to cooperation. We are honored in being given the opportunity to participate in His good deeds. Remember how He asked for help in performing His miracles: Fill the water pots, stretch out your hand, distribute the loaves.

Elisabeth Elliot

42

God does not need our money. But, you and I need the experience of giving it.

James Dobson

The mark of a Christian is that he will walk the second mile and turn the other cheek. A wise man or woman gives the extra effort, all for the glory of the Lord Jesus Christ.

John Maxwell

Love Is Generous

God does not supply money to satisfy our every whim and desire. His promise is to meet our needs and provide an abundance so that we can help other people.

Larry Burkett

When somebody needs a helping hand, he doesn't need it tomorrow or the next day. He needs it now, and that's exactly when you should offer to help. Good deeds, if they are really good, happen sooner rather than later.

Marie T. Freeman

Two works of mercy set a man free: forgive and you will be forgiven, and give and you will receive.

St. Augustine

love

When it is in your power, don't withhold good from the one to whom it is due.

Proverbs 3:27 HCSB

44

So whenever you give to the poor, don't sound a trumpet before you, as the hypocrites do in the synagogues and on the streets, to be applauded by people. I assure you: They've got their reward! But when you give to the poor, don't let your left hand know what your right hand is doing, so that your giving may be in secret. And your Father who sees in secret will reward you.

Matthew 6:2-4 HCSB

A generous person will be enriched.

Proverbs 11:25 HCSB

Love Is Generous

So He called His disciples to Himself and said to them, "Assuredly, I say to you that this poor widow has put in more than all those who have given to the treasury; for they all put in out of their abundance, but she out of her poverty put in all that she had, her whole livelihood."

Mark 12:43-44 NKJV

Assuredly, I say to you, inasmuch as you did it to one of the least of these My brethren, you did it to Me.

Matthew 25:40 NKJV

Freely you have received, freely give.

Matthew 10:8 NKJV

46

If you want to be truly happy,
you won't find it on an endless quest
for more stuff.
You'll find it in receiving God's generosity
and in passing that generosity along.

—

Bill Hybels

Chapter 5

Friends

I give thanks to my God for every remembrance of you.

—

Philippians 1:3 HCSB

Friend: a one-syllable word describing "a person who is attached to another by feelings of affection or personal regard." This definition, or one very similar to it, can be found in any dictionary, but genuine friendship is much more. When we examine the deeper meaning of friendship, so many descriptors come to mind: trustworthiness, loyalty, helpfulness, kindness, understanding, forgiveness, encouragement, humor, and cheerfulness, to mention but a few.

Genuine friendship should be treasured and nurtured. As Christians, we are commanded to love one another. The familiar words of 1 Corinthians 13:2 remind us that love and charity are among God's greatest gifts: "And though I have the gift of prophecy, and understand all mysteries, and all knowledge; and though I have all faith, so that I could remove mountains, and have not charity, I am nothing" (KJV).

48

Friends

Today and every day, resolve to be a trustworthy, encouraging, loyal friend. And, treasure the people in your life who are loyal friends to you. Friendship is, after all, a glorious gift, praised by God. Give thanks for that gift and nurture it.

49

In friendship,
God opens your eyes to the glories of Himself.

—

Joni Eareckson Tada

Do you want to be wise? Choose wise friends.

Charles Swindoll

Don't bypass the potential for meaningful friendships just because of differences. Explore them. Embrace them. Love them.

Luci Swindoll

50

Yes, the Spirit was sent to be our Counselor. Yes, Jesus speaks to us personally. But often he works through another human being.

John Eldredge

Live in the present and make the most of your opportunities to enjoy your family and friends.

Barbara Johnson

Friends

God often keeps us on the path by guiding us through the counsel of friends and trusted spiritual advisors.

Bill Hybels

We long to find someone who has been where we've been, who shares our fragile skies, who sees our sunsets with the same shades of blue.

Beth Moore

Friendship is one of the sweetest joys of life. Many might have failed beneath the bitterness of their trial had they not found a friend.

C. H. Spurgeon

A friend is one who makes me do my best.

Oswald Chambers

A friend loveth at all times, and a brother is born for adversity.

Proverbs 17:17 KJV

Oil and incense bring joy to the heart, and the sweetness of a friend is better than self-counsel.

52

Proverbs 27:9 HCSB

Beloved, if God so loved us, we also ought to love one another.

1 John 4:11 NKJV

Friends

A friend loves at all times, and a brother is born for a difficult time.

Proverbs 17:17 HCSB

Thine own friend, and thy father's friend, forsake not....

Proverbs 27:10 KJV

The one who loves his brother remains in the light, and there is no cause for stumbling in him.

1 John 2:10 HCSB

Finally, all of you be of one mind, having compassion for one another; love as brothers, be tenderhearted, be courteous.

1 Peter 3:8 NKJV

54

Perhaps the greatest treasure on earth and
one of the only things that will survive this
life is human relationships: old friends.
We are indeed rich if we have friends.
Friends who have loved us through
the problems and heartaches of life.
Deep, true, joyful friendships.
Life is too short and eternity too long
to live without old friends.

—

Gloria Gaither

Chapter 6

Spending Time
with Loved Ones

He has made everything appropriate in its time.
He has also put eternity in their hearts, but man cannot discover
the work God has done from beginning to end.

—

Ecclesiastes 3:11 HCSB

I t takes time to build strong relationships . . . lots of time. Yet we live in a world where time seems to be an ever-shrinking commodity as we rush from place to place with seldom a moment to spare.

Has the busy pace of life robbed you of sufficient time with your loved ones? If so, it's time to adjust your priorities. And God can help.

56

When you fervently ask God to you help prioritize your life, He will give you guidance. When you seek His guidance every day, your Creator will reveal Himself in a variety of ways. As a follower of Christ, you must do no less.

When you allow God to help you organize your day, you'll soon discover that there is ample time for yourself and your family. When you make God a full partner in every aspect of your life, He will lead you along the proper path: His path. When you allow God to reign over your heart, He will honor you with spiritual blessings that are simply too numerous to count. So, as you plan for the day ahead, make God's priorities your priorities. When you do, every other priority will have a tendency to fall neatly into place.

57

The best use of life is love.
The best expression of love is time.
The best time to love is now.

—

Rick Warren

Frustration is not the will of God. There is time to do anything and everything that God wants us to do.

Elisabeth Elliot

58

Our leisure, even our play, is a matter of serious concern. There is no neutral ground in the universe: every square inch, every split second, is claimed by God and counterclaimed by Satan.

C. S. Lewis

God has a present will for your life. It is neither chaotic nor utterly exhausting. In the midst of many good choices vying for your time, He will give you the discernment to recognize what is best.

Beth Moore

Spending Time with Loved Ones

As we surrender the use of our time to the lordship of Christ, He will lead us to use it in the most productive way imaginable.

Charles Stanley

Our time is short! The time we can invest for God, in creative things, in receiving our fellowmen for Christ, is short!

Billy Graham

The work of God is appointed. There is always enough time to do the will of God.

Elisabeth Elliot

Therefore humble yourselves under the mighty hand of God, that He may exalt you in due time.

1 Peter 5:6 NKJV

He said to them, "It is not for you to know times or periods that the Father has set by His own authority."

Acts 1:7 HCSB

60

I wait for the Lord, my soul waits, and in His word I do hope. My soul waits for the Lord more than those who watch for the morning— Yes, more than those who watch for the morning.

Psalm 130:5-6 NKJV

Spending Time with Loved Ones

Therefore the Lord is waiting to show you mercy, and is rising up to show you compassion, for the Lord is a just God. Happy are all who wait patiently for Him.

Isaiah 30:18 HCSB

But those who wait on the LORD shall renew their strength; they shall mount up with wings like eagles, they shall run and not be weary, they shall walk and not faint.

Isaiah 40:31 NKJV

For My thoughts are not your thoughts, and your ways are not My ways. For as heaven is higher than earth, so My ways are higher than your ways, and My thoughts than your thoughts.

Isaiah 55:8-9 HCSB

62

Overcommitment and time pressures are
the greatest destroyers of marriages
and families. It takes time to develop
any friendship, whether with a loved one
or with God himself.

—

James Dobson

Chapter 7

The Power of Encouragement

*I want their hearts to be encouraged and joined together in love,
so that they may have all the riches of assured understanding,
and have the knowledge of God's mystery—Christ.*

—

Colossians 2:2 HCSB

In the Book of Proverbs, we read that, "A word spoken at the right time is like golden apples on a silver tray" (25:11 HCSB). This verse reminds us that the words we speak can and should be beautiful offerings to those we love.

All of us have the power to enrich the lives of our loved ones. Sometimes, when we feel uplifted and secure, we find it easy to speak words of encouragement and hope. Other times, when we are discouraged or tired, we can scarcely summon the energy to uplift ourselves, much less anyone else. But, as loving Christians, our obligation is clear: we must always measure our words carefully as we use them to benefit others and to glorify our Father in heaven.

God intends that we speak words of kindness, wisdom, and truth, no matter our circumstances, no matter our emotions. When we do, we share a priceless gift with our loved ones, and we give glory to the One who gave His life for us. As believers, we must do no less.

He climbs highest who helps another up.

Zig Ziglar

No journey is complete that does not lead through some dark valleys. We can properly comfort others only with the comfort we ourselves have been given by God.

65

Vance Havner

To the loved, a word of affection is a morsel, but to the love-starved, a word of affection can be a feast.

Max Lucado

God of our life, there are days when the burdens we carry chafe our shoulders and weigh us down; when the road seems dreary and endless, the skies gray and threatening; when our lives have no music in them, and our hearts are lonely, and our souls have lost their courage. Flood the path with light, run our eyes to where the skies are full of promise; tune our hearts to brave music; give us the sense of comradeship with heroes and saints of every age; and so quicken our spirits that we may be able to encourage the souls of all who journey with us on the road of life, to Your honor and glory.

St. Augustine

The balance of affirmation and discipline, freedom and restraint, encouragement and warning is different for each child and season and generation, yet the absolutes of God's Word are necessary and trustworthy at all times.

Gloria Gaither

The Power of Encouragement

Encouragement starts at home, but it should never end there.

Marie T. Freeman

One of the ways God refills us after failure is through the blessing of Christian fellowship. Just experiencing the joy of simple activities shared with other children of God can have a healing effect on us.

Anne Graham Lotz

We can never untangle all the woes in other people's lives. We can't produce miracles overnight. But we can bring a cup of cool water to a thirsty soul, or a scoop of laughter to a lonely heart.

Barbara Johnson

Carry one another's burdens; in this way you will fulfill the law of Christ.

Galatians 6:2 HCSB

But encourage each other daily, while it is still called today, so that none of you is hardened by sin's deception.

Hebrews 3:13 HCSB

And let us be concerned about one another in order to promote love and good works.

Hebrews 10:24 HCSB

The Power of Encouragement

Anxiety in a man's heart weighs it down, but a good word cheers it up.

Proverbs 12:25 HCSB

Iron sharpens iron, and one man sharpens another.

Proverbs 27:17 HCSB

Avoid irreverent, empty speech, for this will produce an even greater measure of godlessness.

2 Timothy 2:16 HCSB

If anyone thinks he is religious, without controlling his tongue but deceiving his heart, his religion is useless.

James 1:26 HCSB

70

What are your spouse's dreams?
What are you doing to encourage
or discourage those dreams?

—

Dennis Swanberg

Chapter 8

Love and Laughter

*There is an occasion for everything, and a time for every activity
under heaven . . . a time to weep and a time to laugh;
a time to mourn and a time to dance.*

—

Ecclesiastes 3:1, 4 HCSB

Laughter is a gift from God, a gift that He intends for us to use. Yet sometimes, because of the inevitable stresses of everyday living, we fail to find the fun in life. When we allow life's inevitable disappointments to cast a pall over our lives and our souls, we do a profound disservice to ourselves and to our loved ones.

If you've allowed the clouds of life to obscure the blessings of life, perhaps you've formed the unfortunate habit of taking things just a little too seriously. If so, it's time to fret a little less and laugh a little more.

So today, look for the humor that most certainly surrounds you and your loved ones. Remember: God created laughter for a reason...and Father indeed knows best. So laugh!

Love and Laughter

When we bring sunshine into the lives of others, we're warmed by it ourselves. When we spill a little happiness, it splashes on us.

Barbara Johnson

We may run, walk, stumble, drive, or fly, but let us never lose sight of the reason for the journey, or miss a chance to see a rainbow on the way.

Gloria Gaither

The people whom I have seen succeed best in life have always been cheerful and hopeful people who went about their business with a smile on their faces.

Charles Kingsley

Christ can put a spring in your step and a thrill in your heart. Optimism and cheerfulness are products of knowing Christ.

Billy Graham

74

If you want people to feel comfortable around you, to enjoy being with you, then learn to laugh at yourself and find humor in life's little mishaps.

Dennis Swanberg

I think everybody ought to be a laughing Christian. I'm convinced that there's just one place where there's not any laughter, and that's hell.

Jerry Clower

Love and Laughter

Laughter is to life what shock absorbers are to automobiles. It won't take the potholes out of the road, but it sure makes the ride smoother.

Barbara Johnson

It is pleasing to the dear God whenever you rejoice or laugh from the bottom of your heart.

Martin Luther

If you can laugh at yourself loudly and often, you will find it liberating. There's no better way to prevent stress from becoming distress.

John Maxwell

It is often just as sacred to laugh as it is to pray.

Charles Swindoll

A joyful heart makes a face cheerful.

Proverbs 15:13 HCSB

76

Oh, clap your hands, all you peoples! Shout to God with the voice of triumph!

Psalm 47:1 NKJV

And not only so, but we also joy in God through our Lord Jesus Christ, by whom we have now received the atonement.

Romans 5:11 KJV

Love and Laughter

The Lord reigns; let the earth rejoice.

Psalm 97:1 NKJV

I will thank the Lord with all my heart; I will declare all Your wonderful works. I will rejoice and boast about You; I will sing about Your name, Most High.

Psalm 9:1-2 HCSB

My lips will shout for joy when I sing praise to You.

Psalm 71:23 HCSB

78

A little comic relief in a discussion does
no harm, however serious the topic may be.
(In my own experience the funniest things
have occurred in the gravest
and most sincere conversations.)

—

C. S. Lewis

Chapter 9

Love Requires Patience

A patient spirit is better than a proud spirit.

—

Ecclesiastes 7:8 HCSB

L oving relationships inevitably require patience . . . plenty of patience.

We live in an imperfect world inhabited by imperfect people, and we need to be patient with everybody, especially our loved ones. Most of us, however, are perfectly willing to be patient with our spouses just as long as things unfold according to our own plans and according to our own timetables. In other words, we know precisely what we want, and we know precisely when we want it: right now, if not sooner.

As the old saying goes, "God gave everyone patience—wise people use it." But, for most of us, being patient with other folks is difficult. Why? Because we (like the "other folks") are fallible human beings, sometimes quick to anger and sometimes slow to forgive.

The next time you find your patience tested to the limit, slow down, calm down, and pray for guidance. And remember this: sometimes, we must wait patiently for our loved ones, and sometimes we must wait patiently for God. And that's as it should be. After all, think how patient God has been with us.

81

Those who have had to wait and work
for happiness seem to enjoy it more,
because they never take it for granted.

—

Barbara Johnson

Waiting is an essential part of spiritual discipline. It can be the ultimate test of faith.

Anne Graham Lotz

God never hurries. There are no deadlines against which He must work. To know this is to quiet our spirits and relax our nerves.

A. W. Tozer

The deepest spiritual lessons are not learned by His letting us have our way in the end, but by His making us wait, bearing with us in love and patience until we are able honestly to pray what He taught His disciples to pray: Thy will be done.

Elisabeth Elliot

Love Requires Patience

Waiting means going about our assigned tasks, confident that God will provide the meaning and the conclusions.

Eugene Peterson

No matter what we are going through, no matter how long the waiting for answers, of one thing we may be sure. God is faithful. He keeps His promises. What He starts, He finishes... including His perfect work in us.

Gloria Gaither

It is wise to wait because God gives clear direction only when we are willing to wait.

Charles Stanley

Now we exhort you, brethren, warn those who are unruly, comfort the faithhearted, uphold the weak, be patient with all.

1 Thessalonians 5:14 NKJV

84 *For ye have need of patience, that, after ye have done the will of God, ye might receive the promise.*

Hebrews 10:36 KJV

Therefore the Lord is waiting to show you mercy, and is rising up to show you compassion, for the Lord is a just God. Happy are all who wait patiently for Him.

Isaiah 30:18 HCSB

Love Requires Patience

My dearly loved brothers, understand this: everyone must be quick to hear, slow to speak, and slow to anger, for man's anger does not accomplish God's righteousness.

James 1:19-20 HCSB

A patient person [shows] great understanding, but a quick-tempered one promotes foolishness.

Proverbs 14:29 HCSB

A person's insight gives him patience, and his virtue is to overlook an offense.

Proverbs 19:11 HCSB

86

If you want to hear God's voice clearly
and you are uncertain, then remain in
His presence until He changes that
uncertainty. Often much can happen
during this waiting for the Lord.
Sometimes he changes pride into humility;
doubt into faith and peace....

—

Corrie ten Boom

Chapter 10

Love Requires Truth

You will know the truth, and the truth will set you free.

—

John 8:32 HCSB

Great relationships are built on a foundation of trust. Without trust, relationships of every kind tend to wither on the vine; with trust, relationships don't just grow; they flourish.

It's been said on many occasions that honesty is the best policy. For believers, it's far more important to note that honesty is God's policy. And, if we are to be servants worthy of our Savior, Jesus Christ, we must be honest and forthright in all our communications with all people, starting with our loved ones. God's Word is clear: "Lying lips are an abomination to the Lord, but those who deal truthfully are His delight" (Proverbs 12:22 NKJV).

In the Book of Exodus, God did not command, "Thou shalt not bear false witness when it is convenient." And He didn't say, "Thou shalt not bear false witness most of the time." God said, "Thou shalt not bear false witness" period—no "ifs, ands, or buts."

Love Requires Truth

Sometime soon, perhaps even today, you will be tempted to start monkeyin' with the truth . . . you know what I mean: to bend it, stretch it, shape it, or break it. Resist that temptation. Truth is God's way...and it must be your way, too.

Do you want relationships that can stand the test of time? Then build your relationships upon mutual trust and unerring truth. It's the only decent way to love.

Truth is always about something,
but reality is that about which truth is.

—

C. S. Lewis

We have in Jesus Christ a perfect example of how to put God's truth into practice.

Bill Bright

For Christians, God himself is the only absolute; truth and ethics are rooted in his character.

Charles Colson

90

Truth will triumph. The Father of truth will win, and the followers of truth will be saved.

Max Lucado

Only Jesus Christ is the truth for everyone who has ever been born into the human race, regardless of culture, age, nationality, generation, heritage, gender, color, or language.

Anne Graham Lotz

Love Requires Truth

Those who walk in truth walk in liberty.

Beth Moore

Having a doctrine pass before the mind is not what the Bible means by knowing the truth. It's only when it reaches down deep into the heart that the truth begins to set us free, just as a key must penetrate a lock to turn it, or as rainfall must saturate the earth down to the roots in order for your garden to grow.

John Eldredge

If the price of which you shall have a true experience is that of sorrow, buy the truth at that price.

C. H. Spurgeon

You are a king then? Pilate asked. "You say that I'm a king," Jesus replied. "I was born for this, and I have come into the world for this: to testify to the truth. Everyone who is of the truth listens to My voice."

John 18:37 HCSB

92

These are the things you must do: Speak truth to one another; render honest and peaceful judgments in your gates.

Zechariah 8:16 HCSB

Be diligent to present yourself approved to God, a worker who doesn't need to be ashamed, correctly teaching the word of truth.

2 Timothy 2:15 HCSB

Love Requires Truth

You have already heard about this hope in the message of truth, the gospel that has come to you. It is bearing fruit and growing all over the world, just as it has among you since the day you heard it and recognized God's grace in the truth.

Colossians 1:5-6 HCSB

For God's wrath is revealed from heaven against all godlessness and unrighteousness of people who by their unrighteousness suppress the truth.

Romans 1:18 HCSB

I have no greater joy than this: to hear that my children are walking in the truth.

3 John 1:4 HCSB

94

The best evidence of our having the truth is
our walking in the truth.

—

Matthew Henry

Chapter 11

Praying for Our Loved Ones

The intense prayer of the righteous is very powerful.

—

James 5:16 HCSB

J esus made it clear to His disciples: they should pray always. And so should we. Genuine, heartfelt prayer changes things and it changes us. When we lift our hearts to our Father in heaven, we open ourselves to a never-ending source of divine wisdom, limitless power, and infinite love.

Today, we offer a prayer of thanks to God for our loved ones. Loyal Christian friends and family members have much to offer us: encouragement, faith, fellowship, and fun, for starters. And when we align ourselves with godly believers, we are blessed by them and by our Creator.

Let us thank God for all the people who love us—for the people He has placed along our paths. And let's pray for our family and friends with sincere hearts. God hears our prayers, and He responds.

Praying for Our Loved Ones

A life growing in its purity and devotion will be a more prayer-ful life.

E. M. Bounds

God knows that we, with our limited vision, don't even know that for which we should pray. When we entrust our requests to him, we trust him to honor our prayers with holy judg-ment.

Max Lucado

Prayer guards hearts and minds and causes God to bring peace out of chaos.

Beth Moore

Two wings are necessary to lift our souls toward God: prayer and praise. Prayer asks. Praise accepts the answer.

Mrs. Charles E. Cowman

Find a place to pray where no one imagines that you are praying. Then, shut the door and talk to God.

Oswald Chambers

98

Prayer connects us with God's limitless potential.

Henry Blackaby

To pray is to mount on eagle's wings above the clouds and get into the clear heaven where God dwells.

C. H. Spurgeon

Praying for Our Loved Ones

We forget that God sometimes has to say "No." We pray to Him as our heavenly Father, and like wise human fathers, He often says, "No," not from whim or caprice, but from wisdom, from love, and from knowing what is best for us.

Peter Marshall

I learned as never before that persistent calling upon the Lord breaks through every stronghold of the devil, for nothing is impossible with God. For Christians in these troubled times, there is simply no other way.

Jim Cymbala

What of the great prayer Jesus taught us to pray? It is for His kingdom and His will, yet we ought not to ask it unless we ourselves are prepared to cooperate.

Elisabeth Elliot

Let the words of my mouth and the meditation of my heart be acceptable in Your sight, O Lord, my strength and my Redeemer.

Psalm 19:14 NKJV

Yet He often withdrew to deserted places and prayed.

Luke 5:16 HCSB

100

Don't worry about anything, but in everything, through prayer and petition with thanksgiving, let your requests be made known to God.

Philippians 4:6 HCSB

Rejoice in hope; be patient in affliction; be persistent in prayer.

Romans 12:12 HCSB

Praying for Our Loved Ones

And everything—whatever you ask in prayer, believing—you will receive.

Matthew 21:22 HCSB

Rejoice always! Pray constantly. Give thanks in everything, for this is God's will for you in Christ Jesus.

1 Thessalonians 5:16-18 HCSB

Therefore I want the men in every place to pray, lifting up holy hands without anger or argument.

1 Timothy 2:8 HCSB

102

Only God can move mountains,
but faith and prayer can move God.

—

E. M. Bounds

Chapter 12

Love Requires Forgiveness

Then Jesus said, "Father, forgive them, for they do not know what they do." And they divided His garments and cast lots.

—

Luke 23:34 NKJV

How often must we forgive family members and friends? More times than we can count. Our children are precious but imperfect; so are our spouses and our friends. We must, on occasion, forgive those who have injured us; to do otherwise is to disobey God.

Are you easily frustrated by the inevitable imperfections of others? Are you a prisoner of bitterness and regret? If so, perhaps you need a refresher course in the art of forgiveness.

If there exists even one person, alive or dead, whom you have not forgiven (and that includes yourself), follow God's commandment and His will for your life: forgive. Bitterness, anger, and regret are not part of God's plan for your life. Forgiveness is.

Love Requires Forgiveness

As you have received the mercy of God by the forgiveness of sin and the promise of eternal life, thus you must show mercy.

Billy Graham

Only the truly forgiven are truly forgiving.

C. S. Lewis

Our relationships with other people are of primary importance to God. Because God is love, He cannot tolerate any unforgiveness or hardness in us toward any individual.

Catherine Marshall

Forgiveness is not an emotion. Forgiveness is an act of the will, and the will can function regardless of the temperature of the heart.

Corrie ten Boom

Revenge is the raging fire that consumes the arsonist.

Max Lucado

The more you practice the art of forgiving, the quicker you'll master the art of living.

Marie T. Freeman

Our forgiveness toward others should flow from a realization and appreciation of God's forgiveness toward us.

Franklin Graham

Love Requires Forgiveness

To hold on to hate and resentments is to throw a monkey wrench into the machinery of life.

E. Stanley Jones

I firmly believe a great many prayers are not answered because we are not willing to forgive someone.

D. L. Moody

It is better to forgive and forget than to resent and remember.

Barbara Johnson

When they persisted in questioning Him, He stood up and said to them, "The one without sin among you should be the first to throw a stone at her."

John 8:7 HCSB

And forgive us our sins, for we ourselves also forgive everyone in debt to us.

Luke 11:4 HCSB

Do not judge, and you will not be judged. Do not condemn, and you will not be condemned. Forgive, and you will be forgiven.

Luke 6:37 HCSB

And whenever you stand praying, if you have anything against anyone, forgive him, so that your Father in heaven may also forgive you your wrongdoing.

Mark 11:25 HCSB

Love Requires Forgiveness

Then Peter came to Him and said, "Lord, how many times could my brother sin against me and I forgive him? As many as seven times?" "I tell you, not as many as seven," Jesus said to him, "but 70 times seven."

Matthew 18:21-22 HCSB

And be kind to one another, tenderhearted, forgiving one another, just as God in Christ forgave you.

Ephesians 4:32 NKJV

You have heard that it was said, You shall love your neighbor and hate your enemy. But I tell you, love your enemies, and pray for those who persecute you, so that you may be sons of your Father in heaven.

Matthew 5:43-45 HCSB

110

God expects us to forgive others
as He has forgiven us;
we are to follow His example
by having a forgiving heart.

—

Vonette Bright

Chapter 13

Growing Together

But grow in the grace and knowledge of our Lord and Savior Jesus Christ. To Him be the glory both now and to the day of eternity.

—

2 Peter 3:18 HCSB

As Christians, we can—and should—never stop growing in the love and knowledge of our Savior.

When we cease to grow, either emotionally or spiritually, we do ourselves and our loved ones a profound disservice. But, if we study God's Word, if we obey His commandments, and if we live in the center of His will, we will not be "stagnant" believers; we will, instead, be growing Christians . . . and that's exactly what God wants for our lives and our relationships.

Many of life's most important lessons are painful to learn. Thankfully, during times of heartbreak and hardship, God stands ready to protect us. As Psalm 46:1 promises, "God is our protection and our strength. He always helps in times of trouble" (NCV). In His own time and according to His master plan, God will heal us if we invite Him into our hearts.

Spiritual growth need not take place only in times of adversity. We must seek to grow in our knowledge and love of the Lord every day that we live. In those quiet moments when we open our hearts to God, the One who made us keeps re-making us. He gives us direction, perspective, wisdom, and courage. And, the appropriate moment to accept those spiritual gifts is always the present one.

113

I'm not what I want to be.
I'm not what I'm going to be.
But, thank God, I'm not what I was!

—

Gloria Gaither

Some people have received Christ but have never reached spiritual maturity. We should grow as Christians every day, and we are not completely mature until we live in the presence of Christ.

Billy Graham

We had plenty of challenges, some of which were tremendously serious, yet God has enabled us to walk, crawl, limp, or leap—whatever way we could progress—toward wholeness.

Beth Moore

Growth in depth and strength and consistency and fruitfulness and ultimately in Christlikeness is only possible when the winds of life are contrary to personal comfort.

Anne Graham Lotz

Growing Together

Recently I've been learning that life comes down to this: God is in everything. Regardless of what difficulties I am experiencing at the moment, or what things aren't as I would like them to be, I look at the circumstances and say, "Lord, what are you trying to teach me?"

Catherine Marshall

I've never met anyone who became instantly mature. It's a painstaking process that God takes us through, and it includes such things as waiting, failing, losing, and being misunderstood—each calling for extra doses of perseverance.

Charles Swindoll

I do not know how the Spirit of Christ performs it, but He brings us choices through which we constantly change, fresh and new, into His likeness.

Joni Eareckson Tada

love

For this reason also, since the day we heard this, we haven't stopped praying for you. We are asking that you may be filled with the knowledge of His will in all wisdom and spiritual understanding.

Colossians 1:9 HCSB

116

I want their hearts to be encouraged and joined together in love, so that they may have all the riches of assured understanding, and have the knowledge of God's mystery—Christ.

Colossians 2:2 HCSB

Therefore, leaving the elementary message about the Messiah, let us go on to maturity.

Hebrews 6:1 HCSB

Growing Together

For You, O God, have tested us; You have refined us as silver is refined. You brought us into the net; You laid affliction on our backs. You have caused men to ride over our heads; we went through fire and through water; but You brought us out to rich fulfillment.

Psalm 66:10–12 NKJV

Like newborn infants, desire the unadulterated spiritual milk, so that you may grow by it in your salvation.

1 Peter 2:2 HCSB

For though by this time you ought to be teachers, you need someone to teach you again the basic principles of God's revelation. You need milk, not solid food. Now everyone who lives on milk is inexperienced with the message about righteousness, because he is an infant. But solid food is for the mature—for those whose senses have been trained to distinguish between good and evil.

Hebrews 5:12-14 HCSB

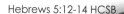

118

Walking in faith brings you to
the Word of God.
There you will be healed, cleansed, fed,
nurtured, equipped, and matured.

—

Kay Arthur

Chapter 14

The Right Words

Pleasant words are a honeycomb:
sweet to the taste and health to the body.

—

Proverbs 16:24 HCSB

All too often, we underestimate the importance of the words we speak. Whether we realize it or not, our words carry great weight and great power, especially when we are addressing our loved ones.

Christ taught that "Out of the abundance of the heart the mouth speaks" (Matthew 12:34 NKJV). Does the abundance of your heart produce a continuing flow of encouraging words for your loved ones? And, are you willing to hold your tongue when you feel the urge to begin an angry outburst? Hopefully so. After all, sometimes the most important words are the ones you don't speak.

If you want to build better relationships—and if you want to keep building them day by day—think first and talk next. Avoid angry outbursts. Refrain from constant criticism. Terminate tantrums. Negate negativism. Cease cynicism. Instead, use Christ as your guide, and speak words of encouragement, hope, praise, and, above all, love—and speak them often.

The Right Words

We should ask ourselves three things before we speak: Is it true? Is it kind? Does it glorify God?

Billy Graham

Fill the heart with the love of Christ so that only truth and purity can come out of the mouth.

Warren Wiersbe

Part of good communication is listening with the eyes as well as with the ears.

Josh McDowell

When you talk, choose the very same words that you would use if Jesus were looking over your shoulder. Because He is.

Marie T. Freeman

Attitude and the spirit in which we communicate are as important as the words we say.

Charles Stanley

122

The fewer words, the better prayer.

Martin Luther

Does your message end with one point like a sword, or does it end like a broom with a thousand straws?

Vance Havner

The Right Words

The great test of a man's character is his tongue.

Oswald Chambers

The things that we feel most deeply we ought to learn to be silent about, at least until we have talked them over thoroughly with God.

Elisabeth Elliot

Change the heart, and you change the speech.

Warren Wiersbe

There is one who speaks rashly, like a piercing sword; but the tongue of the wise [brings] healing.

Proverbs 12:18 HCSB

For the one who wants to love life and to see good days must keep his tongue from evil and his lips from speaking deceit.

1 Peter 3:10 HCSB

Avoid irreverent, empty speech, for this will produce an even greater measure of godlessness.

2 Timothy 2:16 HCSB

No rotten talk should come from your mouth, but only what is good for the building up of someone in need, in order to give grace to those who hear.

Ephesians 4:29 HCSB

The Right Words

If anyone thinks he is religious, without controlling his tongue but deceiving his heart, his religion is useless.

James 1:26 HCSB

Lord, set up a guard for my mouth; keep watch at the door of my lips.

Psalm 141:3 HCSB

I tell you that on the day of judgment people will have to account for every careless word they speak. For by your words you will be acquitted, and by your words you will be condemned.

Matthew 12:36-37 HCSB

Therefore, laying aside all malice, all deceit, hypocrisy, envy, and all evil speaking, as newborn babes, desire the pure milk of the word, that you may grow thereby.

1 Peter 2:1-2 NKJV

126

A little kindly advice is better
than a great deal of scolding.

—

Fanny Crosby

Chapter 15

Your Family

Choose for yourselves today the one you will worship . . . .
As for me and my family, we will worship the Lord.

—

Joshua 24:15 HCSB

loving family is a treasure from God. If God has blessed you with a close knit, supportive clan, offer a word of thanks to your Creator because He has given you one of His most precious earthly possessions. Your obligation, in response to God's gift, is to treat your family in ways that are consistent with His commandments.

128

When you place God squarely in the center of your family's life—when you worship Him, praise Him, trust Him, and love Him—then He will most certainly bless you and yours in ways that you could have scarcely imagined.

So the next time your family life becomes a little stressful, remember this: That little band of men, women, kids, and babies is a priceless treasure on temporary loan from the Father above. And it's your responsibility to praise God for that gift—and to act accordingly.

Your Family

The only true source of meaning in life is found in love for God and his son Jesus Christ, and love for mankind, beginning with our own families.

James Dobson

There is so much compassion and understanding that is gained when we've experienced God's grace firsthand within our own families.

Lisa Whelchel

A home is a place where we find direction.

Gigi Graham Tchividjian

Calm and peaceful, the home should be the one place where people are certain they will be welcomed, received, protected, and loved.

Ed Young

A family is a place where principles are hammered and honed on the anvil of everyday living.

Charles Swindoll

Apart from religious influence, the family is the most important influence on society.

Billy Graham

130

The Golden Rule begins at home.

Marie T. Freeman

I like to think of my family as a big, beautiful patchwork quilt—each of us so different yet stitched together by love and life experiences.

Barbara Johnson

Your Family

Sadly, family problems and even financial problems are seldom the real problem, but often the symptom of a weak or nonexistent value system.

Dave Ramsey

As the first community to which a person is attached and the first authority under which a person learns to live, the family establishes society's most basic values.

Charles Colson

Examine yourselves—ask, each of you, "Have I been a good brother? ...son? ...husband? ...father? ...servant?"

Charles Kingsley

Never give your family the leftovers and crumbs of your time.

Charles Swindoll

If a kingdom is divided against itself, that kingdom cannot stand. If a house is divided against itself, that house cannot stand.

Mark 3:24-25 HCSB

132

The one who brings ruin on his household will inherit the wind.

Proverbs 11:29 HCSB

Unless the Lord builds a house, its builders labor over it in vain; unless the Lord watches over a city, the watchman stays alert in vain.

Psalm 127:1 HCSB

Love must be without hypocrisy. Detest evil; cling to what is good. Show family affection to one another with brotherly love. Outdo one another in showing honor.

Romans 12:9-10 HCSB

133

Do not be unequally yoked together with unbelievers. For what fellowship has righteousness with lawlessness? And what communion has light with darkness?

2 Corinthians 6:14 NKJV

134

The miraculous thing about being a family is
that in the last analysis, we are each
dependent of one another and God,
woven together by mercy given
and mercy received.

—

Barbara Johnson

The Right Kind of Attitude

*Finally brothers, whatever is true, whatever is honorable,
whatever is just, whatever is pure, whatever is lovely,
whatever is commendable—if there is any moral excellence
and if there is any praise—dwell on these things.*

—

Philippians 4:8 HCSB

How will you direct your thoughts today? Will you obey the words of Philippians 4:8 by dwelling upon those things that are honorable, true, and worthy of praise? Or will you allow your thoughts to be hijacked by the negativity that seems to dominate our troubled world? Are you fearful, angry, bored, or worried? Are you so preoccupied with the concerns of this day that you fail to thank God for the promise of eternity? Are you confused, bitter, or pessimistic? If so, God wants to have a little talk with you.

136

God intends that you experience joy and abundance, but He will not force His joy upon you; you must claim it for yourself. So, today and every day hereafter, celebrate this life that God has given you by focusing your thoughts and your energies upon "whatever is of good repute." Today, count your blessings instead of your hardships. And thank the Giver of all things good for gifts that are simply too numerous to count.

The Right Kind of Attitude

Attitude is an inward feeling expressed by behavior.

John Maxwell

It's your choice: you can either count your blessings or re-count your disappointments.

Jim Gallery

The things we think are the things that feed our souls. If we think on pure and lovely things, we shall grow pure and lovely like them; and the converse is equally true.

Hannah Whitall Smith

If the attitude of servanthood is learned, by attending to God as Lord. Then, serving others will develop as a very natural way of life.

Eugene Peterson

138

Life is 10% what happens to you and 90% how you respond to it.

Charles Swindoll

Attitude is the mind's paintbrush; it can color any situation.

Barbara Johnson

The Right Kind of Attitude

The purity of motive determines the quality of action.

Oswald Chambers

The Reference Point for the Christian is the Bible. All values, judgments, and attitudes must be gauged in relationship to this Reference Point.

Ruth Bell Graham

No matter how little we can change about our circumstances, we always have a choice about our attitude toward the situation.

Vonette Bright

"If the Lord will" is not just a statement on a believer's lips; it is the constant attitude of his heart.

Warren Wiersbe

Set your minds on what is above, not on what is on the earth.

Colossians 3:2 HCSB

For the word of God is living and powerful, and sharper than any two-edged sword, piercing even to the division of soul and spirit, and of joints and marrow, and is a discerner of the thoughts and intents of the heart.

140

Hebrews 4:12 NKJV

Make your own attitude that of Christ Jesus.

Philippians 2:5 HCSB

Don't work only while being watched, in order to please men, but as slaves of Christ, do God's will from your heart. Render service with a good attitude, as to the Lord and not to men.

Ephesians 6:6-7 HCSB

The Right Kind of Attitude

May the words of my mouth and the meditation of my heart be acceptable to You, Lord, my rock and my Redeemer.

Psalm 19:14 HCSB

Guard your heart above all else, for it is the source of life.

Proverbs 4:23 HCSB

I, the Lord, examine the mind, I test the heart to give to each according to his way, according to what his actions deserve.

Jeremiah 17:10 HCSB

As for you, Solomon my son, know the God of your father, and serve Him with a whole heart and a willing mind, for the Lord searches every heart and understands the intention of every thought. If you seek Him, He will be found by you, but if you forsake Him, He will reject you forever.

1 Chronicles 28:9 HCSB

love

142

I have witnessed many attitudes
make a positive turnaround
through prayer.

—

John Maxwell

Chapter 17

Sharing the Joy

But let all who take refuge in You rejoice.

—

Psalm 5:11 HCSB

O swald Chambers correctly observed, "Joy is the great note all throughout the Bible." C. S. Lewis echoed that thought when he wrote, "Joy is the serious business of heaven." But, even the most dedicated Christians can, on occasion, forget to celebrate each day for what it is: a priceless gift from God.

Today, let us be joyful Christians with smiles on our faces and kind words on our lips. After all, this is God's day, and He has given us clear instructions for its use. We are commanded to rejoice and be glad. So, with no further ado, let the celebration begin...

If you can forgive the person you were, accept the person you are, and believe in the person you will become, you are headed for joy. So celebrate your life.

Barbara Johnson

The Christian lifestyle is not one of legalistic do's and don'ts, but one that is positive, attractive, and joyful.

Vonette Bright

Joy is the direct result of having God's perspective on our daily lives and the effect of loving our Lord enough to obey His commands and trust His promises.

Bill Bright

Our sense of joy, satisfaction, and fulfillment in life increases, no matter what the circumstances, if we are in the center of God's will.

Billy Graham

146

Joy is the heart's harmonious response to the Lord's song of love.

A. W. Tozer

Lord, I thank you for the promise of heaven and the unexpected moments when you touch my heartstrings with that longing for my eternal home.

Joni Eareckson Tada

Sharing the Joy

God knows everything. He can manage everything, and He loves us. Surely this is enough for a fullness of joy that is beyond words.

Hannah Whitall Smith

God gives to us a heavenly gift called joy, radically different in quality from any natural joy.

Elisabeth Elliot

Rejoice, the Lord is King; Your Lord and King adore! Rejoice, give thanks and sing and triumph evermore.

Charles Wesley

Some of us seem so anxious about avoiding hell that we forget to celebrate our journey toward heaven.

Philip Yancey

Delight yourself also in the Lord, and He shall give you the desires of your heart.

Psalm 37:4 NKJV

148 *Rejoice in the Lord, you righteous ones; praise from the upright is beautiful.*

Psalm 33:1 HCSB

Weeping may endure for a night, but joy comes in the morning.

Psalm 30:5 NKJV

Sharing the Joy

This is the day the Lord has made; let us rejoice and be glad in it.

Psalm 118:24 HCSB

Rejoice in the Lord always. I will say it again: Rejoice!

Philippians 4:4 HCSB

But now I come to You, and these things I speak in the world, that they may have My joy fulfilled in themselves.

John 17:13 NKJV

Glory in His holy name; let the hearts of those rejoice who seek the Lord! Seek the Lord and His strength; seek His face evermore!

1 Chronicles 16:10-11 NKJV

150

A life of intimacy with God is
characterized by joy.

—

Oswald Chambers

Chapter 18

Following Christ

151

Then He said to them all, "If anyone wants to come with Me, he must deny himself, take up his cross daily, and follow Me."

—

Luke 9:23 HCSB

Jesus walks with you. Are you walking with Him? Hopefully, you will choose to walk with Him today and every day of your life.

Jesus loved you so much that He endured unspeakable humiliation and suffering for you. How will you respond to Christ's sacrifice? Will you take up His cross and follow Him (Luke 9:23), or will you choose another path? When you place your hopes squarely at the foot of the cross, when you place Jesus squarely at the center of your life, you will be blessed. If you seek to be a worthy disciple of Jesus, you must acknowledge that He never comes "next." He is always first.

Do you hope to fulfill God's purpose for your life? Do you seek a life of abundance and peace? Do you intend to be Christian, not just in name, but in deed? Then follow Christ. Follow Him by picking up His cross today and every day that you live. When you do, you will quickly discover that Christ's love has the power to change everything, including you.

Jesus makes God visible. But that truth does not make Him somehow less than God. He is equally supreme with God.

Anne Graham Lotz

Jesus was the perfect reflection of God's nature in every situation He encountered during His time here on earth.

Bill Hybels

153

Had Jesus been the Word become word, He would have spun theories about life, but since He was the Word become flesh, He put shoes on all His theories and made them walk.

E. Stanley Jones

Tell me the story of Jesus. Write on my heart every word. Tell me the story most precious, sweetest that ever was heard.

Fanny Crosby

There is not a single thing that Jesus cannot change, control, and conquer because He is the living Lord.

Franklin Graham

The crucial question for each of us is this: What do you think of Jesus, and do you yet have a personal acquaintance with Him?

154

Hannah Whitall Smith

The Word had become flesh, a real human baby. He had not ceased to be God. He was no less God then than before, but He had begun to be man. He was not now God minus some elements of His deity but God plus all that He had made His own by taking manhood to himself.

J. I. Packer

Christians see sin for what it is: willful rebellion against the rulership of God in their lives. And in turning from their sin, they have embraced God's only means of dealing with sin: Jesus.

Kay Arthur

In your greatest weakness, turn to your greatest strength, Jesus, and hear Him say, "My grace is sufficient for you, for My strength is made perfect in weakness" (2 Corinthians 12:9, NKJV).

155

Lisa Whelchel

When you can't see him, trust him. Jesus is closer than you ever dreamed.

Max Lucado

Love consists in this: not that we loved God, but that He loved us and sent His Son to be the propitiation for our sins.

1 John 4:10 HCSB

Therefore if any man be in Christ, he is a new creature: old things are passed away; behold, all things are become new.

2 Corinthians 5:17 KJV

Jesus Christ is the same yesterday, today, and forever.

Hebrews 13:8 HCSB

But we do see Jesus—made lower than the angels for a short time so that by God's grace He might taste death for everyone—crowned with glory and honor because of the suffering of death.

Hebrews 2:9 HCSB

For unto us a Child is born, unto us a Son is given; and the government will be upon His shoulder. And His name will be called Wonderful, Counselor, Mighty God, Everlasting Father, Prince of Peace.

Isaiah 9:6 NKJV

In the beginning was the Word, and the Word was with God, and the Word was God.... And the Word was made flesh, and dwelt among us, (and we beheld his glory, the glory as of the only begotten of the Father,) full of grace and truth.

157

John 1:1, 14 KJV

The next day John saw Jesus coming toward him and said, "Here is the Lamb of God, who takes away the sin of the world!"

John 1:29 HCSB

158

The only source of Life
is the Lord Jesus Christ.

—

Oswald Chambers

Now these three remain: faith, hope, and love.
But the greatest of these is love.

—

1 Corinthians 13:13 HCSB

159